CONTENTS

We need to talk.

When you get down to it, the Bible is the world's greatest love story. Every page is rooted in the story of God's love for the people he created. But God not only longs for us to experience his love but for us to experience deep and genuine love in our marriages. In fact, the intimacy and committed love in a marriage should be a reflection of God's love in our lives.

The Song is a series of materials that i pray will encourage and challenge you in your two most important relationships - your relationship with God first and foremost and the relationship with your spouse being a distant second. Of course these two relationships are in no way mutually exclusive. The foundation of marriage should be a right relationship with God.

That's where this devotional comes in. There are no shortage of marriage books from marriages experts out there. This is not one of those and i am not one of them. Instead my wife and i pray that this will lead you on a spiritual journey that will encourage and challenge your marriage to be all that God has in mind.

I challenge you to carve out a few minutes every day over the next six weeks to sit down together and to use the resource to help you look at your relationship through the lens of God's Word.

We are praying that God would "Awaken Love" in your marriage!

Kyle   *DesiRae*

Kyle & DesiRae Idleman
Southeast Christian Church
Louisville, Kentucky

1 DEEPENING DESIRE

WEEK

DESIRE

DAY 1
I Want to Know What Love Is
Song of Solomon 1:1–3

Where do we go if we want to know what love is? What are the trusted sources to help us understand romantic love? There is certainly no shortage of voices on the subject. The books we read, the music we listen to, and the movies we watch often revolve around the subject of love. Not long ago I was waiting for a prescription to be filled at a local drugstore and decided to kill time in the magazine aisle. The dominant headlines promised answers to all of our questions about love, sex, and relationships. I jotted down some of the headlines:

- What's Love Got to Do with It? (I'm not positive what It is, but It is probably what you think It is.)
- How to Make Her Jealous
- 15 Ways to Get Over a Breakup (#13: cry)
- Why You Must Date a Guy with a Cat (I'll withhold the comments I want to add in an effort to not alienate cat lovers)
- How to Heat Things up Fast
- 60 Tips for Sizzling Sex
- 5 Things You Can Tell about Her in 5 Seconds
- 10 Ways You Know He's Lying

I had too much pride to run the risk of being seen reading any of these magazines. In fact, as I stood in the aisle I pretended to be reading Sports Illustrated in case someone happened to walk by and see me looking at a women's magazine. (That sounds like something a guy who owns a cat would do.) My point is that tons of advice is out there when it comes to our love lives. But if you really want to know what love is and how you can experience it to the fullest, the best source is God's Word. After all, these things were his idea. He is the architect and the creator of love, sex, and marriage, and he know how it works best.

Specifically we will be looking at a book in the Old Testament called Song of Solomon. It may be thousands of years old but its insights about love are up-to-date. It's a book of poetic literature that I pray will do more than just inform you as a husband and wife but inspire you to see the passion and purpose God wants for your marriage relationship.

Song of Solomon as a book of poetry can be romantic and even quite erotic. At times as you are reading Song of Solomon you may find yourself saying, "Wait. What? Who put this into the Bible?" The truth is that the ancient Hebrews didn't label and separate ideas as we do. They didn't have one box for "spiritual stuff" and another for "love stuff," for example. Everything was a spiritual issue, including the mysteries between men and women. We tend to compartmentalize different areas of our lives and we often keep our love lives in a completely separate door from our spiritual lives. We don't often talk about subjects like love, sex, and intimacy in church. But this approach tends to be more of a modern day, Western-culture phenomenon. The people of Solomon's day believed and understood a basic reality: all truth is God's truth. This is where we must begin, with an understanding that God not only has helpful wisdom for our love lives but that these areas fall under his authority. There is no way to know what love is and to experience it fully apart from God.

Let him kiss me with the kisses of his mouth— for your love is more delightful than wine. Pleasing is the fragrance of your perfumes; your name is like perfume poured out. No wonder the young women love you!

– Song of Solomon 1:2–3

Our definition of love can sound a lot like a Hallmark card, but the poetry in Song of Solomon takes us to a different level. The first three verses make it pretty clear that somebody's in love. Though there are some different opinions and interpretations about who says what and to whom through-out this book, these words are thought to be written by Solomon's fiancée; in later verses, the king himself would speak. These words are passion-ate, but look a little closer and you'll find that she spoke of his "name." That's a reference to his character, his reputation. When she heard people speak the name of Solomon, it delighted her because of the kind of person people knew him to be.

The focus of most of those magazines in the drugstore was on physical appearance. And while that is certainly part of attraction (when I first met my wife I didn't think to myself, Look at the character on that girl), if you really want to know what love is, learn to value and admire a person's name. Love should move quickly toward an interest in the true nature of the person.

THE BRIDGE

Today, reflect on the growth of your love during the time you've been together. Where did it really begin for each of you? It may have begun with physical attraction, but when did you first feel that their name was "like perfume poured out"?

When my wife, DesiRae, and I first started dating, I took her to the nursing home to meet my great-grandmother who, at age ninety-four, could be a bit cantankerous at times. I sometimes took my dates there to see how they responded in that environment. Before leaving my great-grandmother's room, I asked her if I could pray for her, and during my prayer I opened my eyes and saw DesiRae holding the hand of my great-grandmother. She suddenly seemed even more beautiful to me (DesiRae, not my great-grandmother . . . not that she wasn't beautiful). Take a few minutes to remember some moments when you were attracted to each other's name.

Here's a cheesy but practical exercise that can help you identify how you are attracted to the "name" of your spouse: Take each letter from your spouse's first name and come up with a character quality you find attractive in them and then share a moment when they demonstrated that quality. Here's what DesiRae came up with for my name:

Kind

Y

Loyal

Encouraging

Apparently the Y was more difficult. I suggested "Yummy" based on Song of Solomon 1:1–3, but she decided to "leave it blank for now." Anyway, have some fun with this. Ask God to deepen your desire for one another by helping you look at each other through this lens.

Next Verse: **Proverbs 22:1**

NOTES:

DAY 2

That's What Makes You Beautiful
Song of Solomon 1:5–6

As the story goes, a few years ago a wife answered the door, and a man asked, "Is this the home of Robert 'Rusty' Stevens, who played Larry Mondello on Leave It to Beaver? We're trying to locate him because we're making a reunion show for the Disney Channel."

She looked at the man as if he were crazy. "This is Robert's home, but I'm afraid he's never been a TV star." Disappointed, the man went away. She was familiar with Beaver's pudgy best buddy, who always had an apple in his back pocket. But her husband Robert? Come on.

"Who was it?" asked Robert. She laughed and told him.
"Oh, he had the right house," he said. "I played Larry in sixty-seven episodes of Leave It to Beaver."
"What? And you never saw fit to mention something like that to me?" Her husband shrugged; no word on whether he pulled a fresh apple out of his pocket and took a bite.

It's probably unlikely that you unknowingly married Topanga or Urkel, but ask yourself how well you really know your spouse. Have you recently taken the time to genuinely ask questions and attentively listen? Some of the best marriage advice I ever received was to become a student of my wife, to intentionally spend my life studying and understanding her. It takes time and effort, but to deepen your desire for your spouse you need to deepen your understanding.

In Song of Solomon 1:5–6, we find Solomon's fiancée not feeling very desirable. Though he may have considered her beautiful, she didn't feel that way about herself. But she felt safe enough to be vulnerable and tell him some things about her that maybe he didn't know.

Dark am I, yet lovely, daughters of Jerusalem, dark like the tents of Kedar, like the tent curtains of Solomon. Do not stare at me because I am dark, because I am darkened by the sun. My mother's sons were angry with me and made me take care of the vineyards; my own vineyard I had to neglect."

—Song of Solomon 1:5–6

In these verses, Solomon's beloved offered a kind of disclaimer. Today it would be, "Please forgive my appearance! I came straight from work." In fact, she was explaining that she was a bit too tanned for the day's standards of glamour. She had been working in the field; she had been serving her family to the neglect of her own needs.

How would that strike you? I would think, Here is a girl who has no sense of entitlement, no pampering. She gets things done and she's willing to break a nail or two doing it. And frankly, I'd find that attractive. It's one of the things I really love about my wife. I remember the first time I held hands with her. We were at the theater watching, The Lion King. She had placed her hand on her leg closest to mine giving me the green light to grab it. I interlocked my fingers with her and noticed right away that her hands were much rougher than mine. I married a farmer's daughter who grew up raising pigs and driving combines. She may have been self-conscious, but I loved these things about her. The more we are genuinely interested in getting to know our spouse, the deeper our desire for them will be. Some of the vulnerability and insecurity that your spouse may be reluctant to share has the power to draw in your heart.

THE BRIDGE

As we've discussed, romantic love may begin with a little eye candy, and that's natural. We're human, and God made us to admire and appreciate beauty. But what are some surprising things you have learned about your spouse along the way that have deepened your desire? What are some of your spouse's insecurities where a few words of encouragement from you might go a long way to make them feel desired? Instead of paying them the same compliments as usual, think through what affirming words they need to hear.

Solomon grew up as the privileged son of a king. His experiences and background were very different from the girl he loved. What are some of the ways God has made you different from your significant other? Instead of assuming that your spouse needs to be more like you, take a few minutes to affirm and value what makes you different.

Next Verse: **Proverbs 31:16–18**

DAY 3
I'll Be There for You
Song of Solomon 1:7

What's your favorite genre of movies to watch?

I read an article that explained the reason we often choose to go to a certain kind of movie is more than just about entertainment. It may be on a subconscious level, but apparently we are drawn to movies that allow us to experience an alternative reality. So if your life is boring and mundane, chances are you love a good action-adventure movie. If your life is safe and comfortable, you may be drawn to a scary movie. If your life is predictable and certain, you may love a good mystery. And if you feel lonely or discon-nected, you may love a romantic tear-jerker or a romantic comedy. (Don't get defensive. I'm not saying these are exclusively the reason you would enjoy a certain kind of movie. Yet there must be some truth to it because I read it on the Internet.)

One of the primary reasons your desire for your spouse diminishes instead of deepens is that you just accept your current reality. You just accept that things are the way they are, and the passionate kisses, the long walks hand-in-hand, and the uncontained laughter are just for the movies. In Song of Solomon we consistently witness the husband and wife pursuing each other and making time together a priority. Here's an example:

Tell me, you whom I love, where you graze your flock

And where you rest your sheep at midday.

Why should I be like a veiled woman beside the flocks of your friends?

– Song of Solomon 1:7

In today's verse, the fiancée made a simple request: Give me your work address. She wanted to know where he hung out during the day, and of course the right question for that was, "Where do you graze your flock?" The point here is not too complicated—she wants to go where he goes. When two people are very much in love, they have no trouble figuring out ways to spend time together. As a matter of fact, time becomes their canvas for creative expressions of love. They try new restaurants or maybe they consistently visit the same one where they order the same thing. They find time and a place to run or take walks. The point is that time together is a priority. The question for you and your spouse may not be, "Where do you graze your flocks?" Instead the questions might sound more like this:

- Do you want to start blocking off Tuesday nights for dinner?
- Do you mind if I run to the grocery store with you?
- Are you free to join me on the porch for a few minutes?
- What if we started going for bike rides in the evening together?
- Do you want to run over and spend some time with your mother?

In struggling marriages, which crumbles first, quality time together or romantic feeling? The answer is yes! Those two things are tightly enmeshed. Time builds love and love makes time. It may come easy when you're head over heels, but in a great marriage it will take a little work. It has to be an intentional priority. You're going to pursue spending time with your spouse because your relationship is worth it. Sometimes we think romantic desire shouldn't require effort, that it should come naturally. But that's not true. Deepening any desire requires time and energy. You make pursuing time with your spouse more of a priority and your feelings of desire will start to catch up with your intentional actions.

Sometimes it's the small stuff that pays the big dividends. He's not really into Downton Abbey, but she likes it—so he sits down and watches with her, sparing the snarky comments. She's not really into watching basketball, but she loves his passion for it. So they watch together (and only talk during the timeouts).

We feel most attracted to people when we see them at their best. I'm impressed with this woman that Solomon loved. She was willing to meet him in the pasture. Not a superromantic place, last time I checked. Sheep do not make for an interesting evening, but she wanted to be where he was.

THE BRIDGE

It's trite to say it, but let's be trite: Love takes time. It takes patience and the willingness to go somewhere—literally or figuratively. For today, let me suggest doing something together out of the normal routine. Find ways to "go" somewhere new, to be together under new circumstances. I'm not so sure about Red Lobster and bowling, but whatever it takes, be there for each other.

Now that our four kids are a bit older, here's how we try to spend time together:
- **Daily**: We take time to talk and pray together without interruptions.
- **Weekly**: We go on a date. We try to go out one evening a week, but sometimes it's just connecting for a short lunch.
- **Quarterly**: We leave town for a two-night romantic getaway (full disclosure: sometimes she comes with me on a work trip).
- **Annually**: Just the two of us go somewhere for a week and have as much fun as possible.

It may look different for you, but I know this doesn't happen by accident. Pull out the calendar and agree together about some times and places where you can connect.

Next Verse: **Ruth 1:16–17**

DAY 4

Shout It Out Loud

Song of Solomon 2:4

I read a story in the news about a billboard off I-95 in North Fort Lauderdale that simply read, "Brad Loves Melissa." Brad had noticed that a jewelry company had a prominent billboard that his wife passed by every day on her commute to work. Over the years Brad has found different ways to publicly declare his love for his wife. He has put the message "Brad Loves Melissa" on everything from a side of a building to a giant inflatable advertising balloon. Brad contacted the jewelry company who owned the billboard and asked for their help in making his declaration of love. Sean Dunn from the jewelry company said, "It was a no-brainer for us, as we are in the business that is all about creating things that show people you love them; 99 percent of the time it is a stunning piece of designer jewelry, but this time it is a billboard."

Can I be honest with you? I don't really like Brad. I don't actually know Brad, but I know enough. He makes the rest of us guys look bad. Can't he just go by the Hallmark store on the night of February 13 like the rest of us? He's like the kid in school who studies for the test and sets the curve high. He's like the neighbor who has a perfect lawn and uses some sort of dark magic to create a checked pattern in his grass. He's making it difficult for the rest of us. The truth is that when it comes to declaring our love for our spouses most of us aren't too proactive or creative.

Solomon and the girl he loves are not shy about their feelings for one another. Like passionate sports fans they want the world to know of their love. There is something about declaring our love that deepens our desire. It's a way of choosing sides and stepping over a line. Solomon's bride-to-be knows how Solomon feels about her, and so does everyone else.

Let him lead me to the banquet hall, and let his banner over me be love.

– Song of Solomon 2:4

Solomon's fiancée spoke of him leading her to the banquet hall. So she likes eating out? Well, that's probably true, but what counts is he's showing her off in public. He takes her hand and says, "I want you to meet the guys." What message does that send? It says, I love you and I want everyone to know it. And she feels special. She says, "Let his banner over me be love." That's what flags are for, right? We wave them to show our allegiance.

Then there's the opposite: that sad situation when people disparage their spouses in public. Both men and women do this, dragging their banner in the mud. Wives dish the dirt about their husbands. Men belittle their wives. And it's all passed off as something light, just joking. "Take my wife— please, take her!"

I've heard Christian leaders speak little one-liners about their wives in sermons. Don't they get it? Marriage is a powerful, sacred bond never to be displayed at half-mast. Real love—well-tended, nurtured love—bears a fierce pride in the objects of our affection. We want to take the ones we love with us wherever we go. And when we're apart, the love still shows.

THE BRIDGE
Look for opportunities to fly your banner in public today. Just be sincere about it, and nobody said you have to rent a billboard or write a love sonnet and post it on Facebook. It doesn't need to be on the scale of a Lifetime movie; just find a simple way to let others know you are excited about your marriage. If nothing else, when you're around some friends or extended family, let your spouse overhear you express your love and admiration for him or her.

Keep this in mind, too: When we say a good word to the world about our marriages, we're saying a good word about marriage itself. In case you haven't noticed, the institution has fallen on hard times in some quarters. People are afraid of becoming another divorce statistic. We could use a few voices that make it clear that marriage is no burden; it's a gift from God that keeps on giving.

Take some time to pray together as a couple and thank Jesus for letting the whole world know of his love for you. When he died for you on the cross, he forever made it clear that his banner over you is love. The more deeply you experience his love, the more deeply you are able to love others.

Next Verse: **James 3:9–12**

NOTES:

DAY 5
Killing Me Softly
Song of Solomon 2:15

I've talked a lot about the positive things we can do to deepen our desire for our spouses, but identifying what detracts from our desire is also important. When you fall in love, you need to address a number of potential challenges to your relationship. When DesiRae and I were first married, we moved into a starter home and, though we had never talked about it, it soon became clear that we had some unspoken and unexpressed expectations of one another. My wife grew up on a farm and the men in her family built their own homes, changed their own oil, and repaired their own leaks. I grew up in a home where I was taught you only needed two tools to fix anything: a telephone and a checkbook. So when things needed to get done, she expected me to fix it, not write a check. Chances are you also married someone who is much different from you.

You face hundreds of issues as a couple. Let me guess: You prefer structure and like to stay organized, but you married someone who is more unstructured and spontaneous? Or what about this? You are a night person but you married a morning person? One of you is more outgoing and loud and the other is more quiet and introverted? Instead of deepening our desire for each other, these inevitable issues have the potential to divide us.

Instead of ignoring our differences and pretending as if they don't exist, we need to identify them and deal with them so the fruit in your marriage, what Solomon called your vineyard, will grow.

Catch for us the foxes, the little foxes that ruin the vineyards, our vineyards that are in bloom. My beloved is mine and I am his; he browses among the lilies.

– Song of Solomon 2:15–16

Solomon's fiancée, who was speaking again, referenced catching foxes in the vineyard. In the Mediterranean climate, grapes have always been plentiful. Growers tend the soil and the vines all year to produce a great crop. But in those days, little foxes snuck in at night and wreaked havoc. Actually, the experts think these "foxes" were more like jackals. They weren't particularly sly—they just liked digging things up and leaving a mess. Maybe they were looking for henhouses.

So she was saying, "Let's hunt down these pests." She was really talking about the little things that uproot relationships. "We're growing something delicious in this vineyard of ours," she was saying, figuratively. "Let's keep watch and lock out the intrusions."

And what are those little relationship varmints? You name it: Bad habits. Issues from the past. Personal flaws that may not seem like much but begin to grate over time. In-laws become outlaws. Intimacy is closeup work—it's going to reveal problems. This is a tough hunt, and it has to be carried out constantly. Guarding your relationship takes vigilance. Are you willing to work at it?

THE BRIDGE
While discussing the little foxes in your relationship, take care! The discussion itself could dig up a few problems. But it's a good idea to do some hunting together; just be sure to agree first on a few rules of grace and patience.

I suggest each of you offers up one fox. She might say, "Sometimes I feel as if your mind is wandering while I'm telling you something important." (At least I think that's what she said.) He might mention some little habit of hers that is bothersome. (I'm not going to tell you; remember yesterday's devotion?) Remember, we're not going after the giants here—Solomon's dad, David, was the one who took on Goliath. Sometimes the devil is in the details.

Don't forget, Solomon's fiancée suggested this hunt in the context of powerful, loving conversation. What happens if you don't do that? You let things build up and then you broach the issue at the worst time and in the worst way.

At that point, the foxes are hunting you.

Next Verse: **Ephesians 4:22–24**

NOTES:

WEEK **2** INCREASING
INTIMACY

INTIMACY

DAY 1
Feels Like the First Time
Song of Solomon 4:10

Did you ever stop to think about that first time? I'm talking about the absolute first time: Adam and Eve.

It had to be awkward, right? He'd never met another woman. She'd never met another man. What did he say to break the ice?

At some point they had to get down to business; God had given them a homework assignment involving multiplication. And when he told them what he wanted, one of them must have said, "Wait—what?"

God had said, "Be fruitful," and they quickly discovered that this was a job for which they wouldn't mind putting in overtime. What would have been obvious to them, that sometimes seems difficult for us to accept, is that sex was God's idea. He didn't just give reluctant permission. He didn't just give a begrudging consent. He blessed the act. I think we too often forget that in this day and age. We think somehow that God and sex don't go together. But make no mistake about it: sex was God's idea. He is the giver of this gift. When we take something that God has called good and treat it like it is dirty and shameful, we offend him as the giver of the gift. It brings pleasure, intimacy, and, of course, it produces children, in accordance with God's plan. He could have made reproduction simple, mechanical, and a joyless act of natural instinct. He could have created sex to feel the same way it feels when your hair grows. But he chose to make it pleasurable.

So much can be said about this subject, but we must agree from the beginning that we are on God's turf. If you begin with the acknowledgement that God created sex, then you will also acknowledge his authority on the subject and accept that he knows how it works best. If you perceive sex as a gift you receive from God, then you will want to enjoy and celebrate it. Song of Solomon passionately and poetically reminds us that sex as prescribed by God is a beautiful and intimate expression of love.

How delightful is your love, my sister, my bride! How much more pleasing is your love than wine, and the fragrance of your perfume more than any spice!

– Song of Solomon 4:10

(The following story is told without the expressed written consent of my parents.) I'll never forget calling my parents at home to wish them a happy anniversary. It was late in the evening when I remembered that this wasn't just any anniversary; it was their fortieth. DesiRae warned me about calling them late in the evening on their anniversary, but I was sure it would be safe. What happened next scars me to this day. I share it now only because my therapist says it will help me heal. My dad picked up the phone, and I said, "Happy anniversary!" Then I sarcastically added, "I hope I'm not interrupting anything." To which my dad replied, "We are just lying in bed reading Song of Solomon to each other." In the background I heard my mom say, "Oh, Ken, he doesn't want to know that." In my mind I immediately hit Ctrl-Alt-Del, but it was too late. The damage was done.

As disturbing as that moment was, there is a reason they were celebrating their marriage by reading Song of Solomon to one another. A celebration of love and intimacy plays out throughout the book. In today's theme verse, Solomon was speaking. We get into the "honeymoon" section of the book, and basically it's a narrative of foreplay. Solomon, as the male, took the lead, just as he should. And notice his punctuation—something I don't recommend during sex, most of the time. So many exclamation marks! Editors tell you not to do that! But Solomon can't help himself!

The groom was taking it all in with his five senses, all of which God made. In the "next verse," below, you'll see that it's a divine command to "rejoice in your wife. Let her tender embrace satisfy you." That's a godly duty we should all be able to get excited about.

THE BRIDGE

I've got a suggestion, and if you find it creepy, that's just one more indication of how far our society has drifted from the original idea of sexuality. My suggestion is that the two of you enjoy the gift of sexuality to its fullest this week and that as you do, you actively thank God for what he has given you in each other—for the way he designed you to physically complete one another. Let God into your sex life—and let sexuality into your God life. I have no idea whether Adam and Eve had an awkward moment, but I do know we need to return to an understanding that God does not shake his head in disgust when husbands and wives enjoy each other. I think he smiles and says, "Yes! I've been looking forward to you finding out about this!"

Why are you still reading? Don't you have some homework to do?

Next Verse: **Genesis 2:24**

NOTES:

_____

_____

_____

_____

_____

_____

_____

_____

_____

_____

DAY 2
Let's Get Physical
Song of Solomon 4:1, 4, 7

For a while I subscribed to a men's health magazine. I signed up to receive the publication in hopes it would keep me inspired to get in shape. Instead, every month when it showed up in the mail, I was filled with guilt and shame for not working out. I also discovered that these magazines have a lot of sex advice. Usually the title of the article was something along the lines of "Six Steps to Sizzling Sex." The sexually explicit articles focused mostly on sexual technique and were quite technical, focusing on where to touch and how to move. Women's magazines take a similar approach. Here's the headline on the cover of one such magazine that caught my eye: "We have the wall-shaking, earth-quaking moves that'll make your bed end up across the room."

Though it's often couched in poetic language, Song of Solomon would certainly be considered sexually explicit. However, it's sexually explicit in a different way than we are used to. Song of Solomon doesn't focus on technique and position. Instead it helps us understand that sexual intimacy is much more than a physical act. One Hebrew word for sex is literally translated, "a mingling of the souls."

In chapter 4 we are allowed into the bedroom and we overhear some of what's said between this husband and wife.

Verse 1 begins with Solomon speaking: "How beautiful you are my darling! Oh, how beautiful!" He made sure his wife felt beautiful. There was no reason for her to feel insecure or self-conscious. He continued, "Your eyes behind your veil are doves." Notice where he's looking. Early on in our marriage, my wife accused me of looking at her like a piece of meat on a plate. I would try to talk my way out of it: "Yeah baby, you're Grade A premium cut." But that didn't help.

Solomon continued with his compliments, "Your hair is like a flock of goats descending from the hills of Gilead." So maybe you need to use a different metaphor, but understand that this was an erotic and intimate compliment. It would have been considered inappropriate for a woman to have her hair down in public, so she would have always worn it up. But now, in the presence of her husband, she let her hair down, and as it fell onto her shoulders, he expressed how honored he was to be the man she gave herself to.

In verse 2 he complimented her teeth, probably because she was smiling. They were having fun together. In verses 3 and 4 he spoke of her lips, her temples, and her neck. He was giving her his full attention and paying attention to every detail. And here's his conclusion in verse 7:

You are altogether beautiful, my darling; there is no flaw in you.

– Song of Solomon 4:7

A few observations (pay attention because this will be on the test):
1. Women respond to verbal communication. He expressed how he felt about and how he saw her, and she responded. Husbands, when is the last time you looked your wife in the eyes and told her how beautiful she is to you? Solomon used words to make her feel safe enough to be vulnerable and secure enough to be expressive.
2. Men respond to visual stimulation. Shocker, I know. But clearly the lights were turned on and she had prepared herself for her husband and let him admire her. She didn't walk out in sweats and zit cream and with an annoyed sigh say, "I suppose you want to do something."

THE BRIDGE
Schedule time this week to put this into practice. Wives, I know it can't be this way every time, but spend some time preparing yourself for your husband. Husbands, look your wife in the eyes and express how beautiful she is to you. You may not be a poet like Solomon, but put some thought into this ahead of time and then help her see herself through your eyes.

Next Verse: **Proverbs 5:18–19**

DAY 3
It Takes the Woman in You to Bring Out the Man in Me
Song of Solomon 4:12

Recently I heard about a sociology experiment that took place several years ago in Chicago. The scientists doing the experiment were studying a child's concept of "delayed gratification." If the incentive was strong enough, would the children in this study have the discipline to delay pleasure?

The children were walked into a room where a plate of warm chocolate chip cookies was sitting on a table. The kids were told that if they could sit there for ten minutes without eating the cookies they would get something better. They didn't tell the kids what the "something better" was, so the kids had to trust them. They secretly videotaped the kids sitting in the room with a plate full of warm cookies. Some of the kids showed no restraint and almost immediately ate the cookies. One little boy looked as if he was in pain as he tried to resist the cookies. My favorite was a little girl who lowered her head so that her eyes were peering just over the edge of the table and then stared at the cookies as if she was attempting to taste the cookies with her eyes. Some of the kids poked at the cookies. One of them licked a cookie and then put it back on the plate.

As we get older, I'm not sure we improve much in the area of "delayed gratification." We don't want to put off the pleasure. We want it right now. We microwave our meals. We buy what we want now and worry about paying for it later. And when it comes to sex, we skip the foreplay and get right to the main event. And that's fine, but from time to time we need to intentionally slow things down. It's difficult to microwave intimacy, so take a deep breath and put the cookies back on the plate.

You are a garden locked up, my sister, my bride; you are a spring enclosed, a sealed fountain.

– Song of Solomon 4:12

As you read chapter 4, it becomes clear that Solomon and his bride were not in a hurry. Sex isn't just a means to an end. Husbands especially would do well to take note on how Solomon began with complimenting her eyes and then worked his way down. Some researchers say it takes a man about ninety seconds to be "ready to roll," while a woman may need twenty to thirty minutes to get there.

Song of Solomon 4:12 is a reference to some of the physical distinctions of a woman. But it's also a beautiful analogy of the "secret gardens" of one another's bodies. They are to be "unlocked." That takes time, tenderness, and patient respect. I won't tell you what the "something better" is, but trust me, if you wait ten minutes before eating the cookies, it will be worth it.

THE BRIDGE
Spend some time talking about what makes you different from another. Outside the bedroom and away from the heat of the moment, talk to your spouse about what unlocks your garden. Try to discuss both the physical and emotional elements that will lead to a more intimate sexual experience. We will never unlock all the mysteries of these gardens, but one thing is for certain: We can have a whole lot of fun trying.

Next Verse: **Genesis 5:1–2**

NOTES:

_____

_____

_____

_____

_____

_____

_____

_____

_____

_____

DAY 4
Tell Me What You Want, and I'll Give You What You Need
Song of Solomon 4:16

How many times have you pulled away from the drive-thru of your favorite fast-food restaurant only to open the bag and find they got your order wrong? You said no lettuce, but there is lettuce. You asked for extra ketchup, but there is only one packet. You ordered a large fry, but they gave you a small. It's happened enough to me that I have become cynical and insist on double-checking that I have exactly what I ordered before driving away. When you don't get what you want, where did it go wrong? Most of the time it goes back to when you placed the order. You told them what you expected and apparently they didn't hear you because you got something different. In recent years, however, fast-food places have minimized this problem by placing a screen that displays what you asked for, and then they ask you, "Does everything look right on the screen?" Clear communication solves a lot of problems.

I'm not sure it would be very romantic to have a screen like that for our marriages that we could use to clearly communicate our expectations and desires, but it would certainly help. My wife may say, "Honey would you rub my back?" but I'm thinking, I know what you're really trying to say. Most of us could use a little screen to clear up the miscommunication. Everyone knows the sexual bed can be an emotional minefield. Men and women both make their share of mistakes, sometimes because we can't put things into words and other times because we take the wrong messages from a look or a gesture.

In a very erotic verse, Solomon's bride placed her order:

Awake, north wind, and come, south wind! Blow on my garden, that its fragrance may spread everywhere. Let my beloved come into his garden and taste its choice fruits.

– Song of Solomon 4:16

Communication is huge. Let me say that again in case you weren't paying attention: communication is huge. But when it comes to our sex lives, we have a hard time communicating clearly and listening carefully. Solomon's new bride was telling him, in poetic language, just what she wanted and needed. The north wind was strong, but the south wind was gentle; this woman needed both tough and tender. She welcomed the "strong winds" to come across her garden, but some gentle breezes would be nice too. We need to do more than simply take what we want. We need to pay attention to the needs of our spouse. The irony (and this is true in every part of faith) is that the more we give, the more we receive. Intimacy grows as we nurture one another rather than simply taking selfishly. That requires saying it clearly and listening carefully.

THE BRIDGE

I know—sometimes we want to take a cue from Nike and go with a "just do it" approach to sex. Some things are hard to put into words. We worry that talking about it will make it less sexy and more clinical.

You've got a surprise in store. Intelligent romance is the way to go, my friends! Talk about it. Listen to each other. Then focus on pleasing one another rather than on personal pleasure, and you're going to like how it turns out. There is no I in intimacy. Wait a minute, actually there are two. Maybe there's something to that.

Today, dare to talk about personal needs and ask God to give you the desire to meet the needs of your spouse. One of prayers I pray for the bride and groom whenever I perform a wedding ceremony goes something like this: "God, may their greatest moments of pleasure come not from having their own needs met but by meeting each other's needs." The ideal attitude is expressed in the verses below from Philippians. The way of Christ is always service, always putting one another first—even sexually.

Next Verse: Philippians 2:3–4

DAY 5
Can You Feel the Love Tonight?
Song of Solomon 5:1

It wasn't too many years ago when most of us discovered HD television. "High Definition" changed how we watched TV. That's especially true when you watch live sporting events. It was during this time that a buddy invited me over to his house to watch the Final Four on his new big-screen HDTV. I arrived at his house a few minutes after the game had started. Some of my other buddies were already there. They were all gathered around his new television. Almost immediately I could tell the game wasn't in HD. I pointed this out to my friend and it was clear that some of the other guys had already realized this but didn't want to say anything. Apparently, my friend spent a bunch of money on his HDTV, but didn't spend money on HD programming. He didn't seem to notice or be too concerned. Why? Because he didn't know the difference. He didn't realize what he was missing. I think there is an HD intimacy that many marriages are missing. Couples have settled for a sex life instead of experiencing the much deeper pleasure of a love life. As you read Song of Solomon I hope it opens your eyes to the kind of passionate intimacy God intended for you to share with your spouse.

We read about this couple making love in chapter 4, and then at the beginning of chapter 5 God has something to say. It's the only time God speaks in this book:

Eat, friends, and drink; drink your fill of love.
– Song of Solomon 5:1

Do you want to know how God feels about sex between a husband and wife in a committed marriage? That verse captures it. God is essentially saying, "Do it again!" God's like, "Yeah, that was my idea. You're welcome." He said to this husband and wife, "Keep drinking."

I was teaching Song of Solomon at the church I serve and during this series we encouraged people to email or text questions they were too embarrassed to ask in person. The number one question submitted was, "How often should a Christian couple make love?" It wasn't always worded that way. Sometimes the question was written more like, "How often do we have to have sex?" You can tell how a husband or wife perceives sexual intimacy by how they ask the question. Paul addressed this question in 1 Corinthians 7. He explained that when a man and woman are married the two become one. Therefore the wife's body no longer belongs to her alone but also to her husband. And the husband's body doesn't belong to him alone but also to his wife. At first this idea might sound a bit archaic, but really it's the only way to have true intimacy. We experience true intimacy when we give ourselves completely to our spouse. In doing so we put each other's needs ahead of our own.

The Message paraphrases 1 Corinthians 7:3 this way: "The marriage bed must be a place of mutuality—the husband seeking to satisfy his wife, the wife seeking to satisfy her husband." This is the opposite of how our culture indoctrinates us to think about sex. The cultural approach to sex is all about getting my needs met and my desires satisfied. And husbands, notice the order here: first Paul said you seek to satisfy your wife, and then wives, you seek to satisfy your husband. So men, what if you put the same passion into your love life as you do working on the car? What if you gave your wife the same attention as you do the game? What if you studied her the same as you study the numbers at work? Wives, what if you took the creativity and focus you used to decorate the bedroom and applied that to what happens in the bed? What if you put the same passion into meeting your husband's need as you do meeting the needs of your children? What if you gave him the same kind of attention you give your job?

There is incredible sexual satisfaction in a marriage when two people are selflessly seeking to satisfy each other. That's how you increase the intimacy. That's also how our marriages can model the love and grace of Jesus. We are never more like him than when we serve selflessly and love completely.

THE BRIDGE

Your homework comes straight from God: "Eat, friends, and drink; drink your fill of love."

Next Verse: **1 Corinthians 7:3–5**

NOTES:

WEEK **3** FIGHTING FAIR

FIGHTING

DAY 1

Things We Said Today

Song of Solomon 5:2–3

For fifty-five years they've been married. And it's been a success. Oh, they've had their share of disagreements, but nothing too major. But now, at eighty, she's in poor health. She's not expected to live much longer. She calls her husband in and they talk quietly. "The shoebox," he says. "The one in your closet. Should we open that now?" She tells him to go ahead and bring it.

On their wedding day, so long ago, she showed him the shoebox and said, "We're going to have a great marriage. We'll work at it. We'll love each other. I just ask that you never open this box, or ask about it, until the end." It was sort of an odd request, but he agreed.

Now he opens the box. It holds two little crosses, knit in gold thread, and a roll of bills that totals more than seventy-five thousand dollars. "What's this all about?" he asks.

She says, "Before we were married, I asked my mother what I should do whenever you didn't live up to my expectations. She said, 'Don't fight. Go sit down, knit a gold cross, and then patch things up with your husband.'"

Now he smiles—only two crosses in sixty years? He must have been a great husband. "What about the money?" he asks.

"Oh, every time I made a cross, I sold it for five bucks. Haven't moved these two yet."

I slept but my heart was awake. Listen! My beloved is knocking: "Open to me, my sister, my darling, my dove, my flawless one. My head is drenched with dew, my hair with the dampness of the night." I have taken off my robe—must I put it on again? I have washed my feet—must I soil them again?

– Song of Solomon 5:2–3

I've counseled my share of engaged couples, and their happiness lights up the room. They're on top of the world. The honeymoon is going to last forever. Why not?

But it never does. Something called real life intrudes. Nobody ever plans for the disagreements, the annoyances, the little "down" moments that catch up with one or both of us. How do we handle those? What happens when we don't?

Solomon's romantic journal has been almost giddy up to now. In the fifth chapter, however, the honeymoon was over. What happened? We see images of a marriage out of sync; their rhythms don't match. He came to her bed ready for love, but she was ready for sleep. Later, she was in the mood but he was in the garden—perhaps pouting.

I've been there; so have you. We need to understand that conflict isn't the sign of a struggling marriage. It's the sign of a normal marriage. God is challenging us to work toward wholeness, because that leads to holiness.

THE BRIDGE

If you major on only one truth this week, let it be this one: How you deal with conflict is going to be the key to how you grow as a couple and also as individual followers of Christ. Those "little collisions" are defining moments. The last thing you need to do is put them in a shoebox and hide them in a closet. How we deal with conflict has the power to divide us or draw us closer together.

Today, talk about and pray about your conflict styles as a couple. Which, if either of you, is more confrontational? Which of you will do almost anything to sweep unpleasantness under the rug? What are the principles you need to work on when it comes to navigating a conflict? Don't focus on what you have conflict over, focus on how you deal with conflict. Resist the temptation to tell the other person how they deal with conflict. Be humble, open, and loving as you allow Christ to make your marriage stronger than ever through this discussion.

Next Verse: **Colossians 3:13**

DAY 2
I Can See Clearly Now
Song of Solomon 5:4

Good, you're still reading. I hope last night wasn't too rough. Raise your hand if you skipped the conversation on conflict. So I guess we know how you deal with it.

In 1941, Samuel Booth and Violet Bailey were in love and soon to be married.

Hand in hand, they took a long and leisurely walk one day. They talked about their future together. Then one of them offered a couple of ill-chosen words. You know how it goes—some little thing that came out wrong. Soon a loud argument was raging. Violet got so caught up in her anger that she pulled off her diamond engagement ring and hurled it into the tall grass.

The odd thing is that later nobody could even remember how the war started. You know how that one goes, too. Soon they'd kissed and made up, but they never did find that ring, even after days of searching.

The Booths went on to be married for five decades. Their kids grew up with the tantalizing story of the lost ring. It was crazy! How could Mom throw away something so valuable (and meaningful) in one angry moment?

In 1993, Samuel passed away. Fifteen more years passed and still family members were talking about that ring. Maybe somehow it was still there, buried by a generation of foliage. One of the grandchildren got a bright idea: why not go to the field with a metal detector? Two hours later, he had the famous ring in his hands.

Samuel would have been happy about that. But I have an idea he and Violet had come away with something much better than a diamond. They learned the value of simple perspective. Don't throw away a diamond over something trivial and insignificant. Solomon said in Proverbs 19:11 that it's to your glory to overlook an offense. Paul wrote in 1 Corinthians 13:5 that love keeps no record of wrongs. Much of the conflict we have in marriage begins with something minor and inconsequential. Our pride is wounded and we react with defensiveness or withdraw and play the part of the victim.

How would Solomon deal with conflict in his marriage?

My beloved thrust his hand through the latch-opening; my heart began to pound for him.

– Song of Solomon 5:4

Solomon and his wife were on two different pages. He came to her room and found the door locked. She was half asleep. The man couldn't have been happy about this; he had been thinking about this moment for the better part of the day and was ready to go.

Still, verse 4 doesn't show him pounding down the door. He took it pretty well, really. Thrusting his hand through the latch-opening was his way of saying, "Well, OK—but hey, I love you." And it's no wonder that she changed her mind in short order. But by the time she rushed to the door, he was gone. Proverbs 15:1 tells us that a soft answer turns away anger, but harsh words stir it up. That's a lesson I've learned far too well. How about you?

In our home, we've decided that everybody is entitled to a bad day or even just a bad moment. This was no more than that: an instant in time. It's when your bad moment meets my impatience that all the trouble starts. What would happen if you caught your spouse at the wrong time, you got a snarky remark, and your response was, "OK—but hey, I love you"?

Perspective: It's what allows us to handle the moment with grace. It's what tells us, this isn't what I signed up for. But it will pass quickly. We are worth this, and God is using this.

THE BRIDGE

Today I'm going to challenge you. Are you ready? I want the two of you to revisit the last quarrel you had. Why exactly did it happen? What was the spark? The point of this exercise is to come away with a better understanding of what kinds of moments are the red flags for each of you and what you could do and say to make something beautiful out of what might otherwise become an ugly situation.

One of the things I love the most about Christ is the way he loves us. The more we experience his unconditional love and his underserved grace the more we are able to extend that to each other.

Next Verse: **1 Corinthians 13:4**

DAY 3
Fix You
Song of Solomon 5:9

My wife and I were newly married and had spent only a few nights in our first house. I was unpacking some things from my bachelor days and came across a BB pistol. I was slinging it around doing my best Wyatt Earp impression, but DesiRae was not impressed. She asked me several times to put it up and warned me that it was going to go off. This of course made me want to continue playing with the gun. And then it happened… no, I didn't shoot her. But I did shoot out a window. She couldn't have been more gracious and she made me feel a little less humiliated by telling me we would laugh about it one day. Later that same night I noticed that one of my favorite shirts had bleach spots on it. She had only done one load of laundry in our married life and had managed to ruin the shirt I wore several days a week (I would later learn that this was premeditated rather than accidental). I wasn't happy. I grabbed my shirt and walked in to tell her off. And then I felt it—a cool breeze coming from a hole in the window. Suddenly I decided that the stained shirt wasn't worth mentioning.

Grace is cyclical. When we give it, we get it. But in marriage it's easy to live in a cycle of "ungrace." This is when we make it our jobs to fix the other person. In the marriage counseling I have done over the years, I have discovered that the husband has no trouble telling me what's wrong with his wife and the wife has no trouble telling me what's wrong with her husband. But when it comes to self-diagnosis, they (and we) are often stumped.

In the middle of their misunderstanding and conflict, Solomon's wife asked her friends for some help in finding her beloved. They asked her what made him so special, and that gave her the opportunity to later brag on her husband.

How is your beloved better than others, most beautiful of women?
How is your beloved better than others, that you so charge us?

– Song of Solomon 5:9

A researcher named Dr. John Gottman discovered something amazing. He was interested in the "I'll change you" issues in marriage. He found that 69 percent of the issues couples disagreed on early in marriage don't get fixed later. That means about 70 percent of the time, we'd better find a way to agree to disagree. We're unlikely to "fix" the issue. Chances are that even as you read that your thinking about the ways your spouse will never change rather than ways you will stay the same. So really the issue isn't so much about change as it is acceptance and grace.

So Kimberly is thinking, He's a slob, but he won't be once I'm through with him. Meanwhile, her fiancé, Tyler, is thinking, She's going to love hunting and fishing; she just doesn't know it yet.

If you could pick one worst time to try fixing the other person, what would it be? Yep, in midconflict. Somehow we try it anyway. We wait until something boils to the surface and then we say, "See, that's the whole trouble with you."

A better use of that moment: listen, learn something helpful about your spouse, and do some self-reflection.

THE BRIDGE
Your spouse is not a project to complete but a child of God designed to be a part of God's plan to complete you. Today, try talking about your own tendencies to fall into this trap. And this is important: Do it without pointing out the things you're tempted to fix. This is not a time to start another dispute!

After touching on that, try discussing the things you've come to love about each other since your marriage began. What has surprised you about your spouse? What have you learned about grace through the way your spouse has accepted and loved you?

Listen to what we're taught: "Accept one another, then, just as Christ accepted you, in order to bring praise to God." There's the key. The church is the bride of Christ, and he has accepted us, totally forgiving every flaw, every sin, every evil thing within us. How can the two of you follow his lead? As you pray together, thank him for his acceptance, and claim it as your mandate in marriage.

Next Verse: **Romans 15:7**

NOTES:

DAY 4

Sorry Seems to Be the Hardest Word
Song of Solomon 6:2–3

In Pixar's The Incredibles, a group of superheroes are trying to hang up their capes and settle into family life. It's a tough transition.

One of them, Frozone (the one who zaps bad guys with streams of snow and ice), is in front of the bathroom mirror. He sees a giant robot trudge by the window. Hero time!

Frozone checks his secret lair and finds that his costume is missing. "Honey!" he yells, "Where is my super suit?"
"What?"
"Where is my super suit?" A helicopter crashes outside. It's getting intense. After being pressed on the issue, Mrs. Frozone finally admits putting away the suit. "But I need it," shouts the hero frantically.
"Uh uh," says his wife. "Don't you think about running off to do no derring-do! We've been planning this dinner for two months."
"But the public is in danger—we're talking about the greater good!"
"I am your wife," she says. "I'm the greatest good you're ever gonna get!"

Mrs. Solomon might nod in agreement to Mrs. Frozone's response.

My beloved has gone down to his garden, to the beds of spices, to browse in the gardens and to gather lilies. I am my beloved's and my beloved is mine; he browses among the lilies.
– Song of Solomon 6:2–3

A critical moment comes in every marital argument, just after the dust clears from the first nasty exchange. A reasonable thought crosses your mind. Maybe it's like in the cartoons: a little angel is whispering in your ear, "C'mon, dude, we can't let this stand. Go make things right. Each tick of the clock will make it worse."

But a little devil is on the other shoulder, whispering, "Don't give in! Protect your pride. Set the precedent. She's the one who needs to apologize." What will you do?

What sets us apart as followers of Jesus Christ is not any lack of stumbling — it's what we do next that counts. We're going to make things right: come together, talk it through, and use that cool superpower known as grace. Mrs. Frozone has it right: Your spouse is the greatest good you're ever gonna get. Nothing is more important than unity in marriage. You're going to argue, but you're also going to work through those arguments; God's Spirit is going to knit you even tighter; and you'll be a stronger couple than before. Marital invulnerability is another superpower.

Notice how we all have our styles of dealing with ill feelings. Solomon had his garden, and his wife knew she'd find him there. I've known people like that. Go to where your spouse is—not just geographically, but emotionally. Be empathic. Listen more deeply, and understand why the argument happened.

THE BRIDGE
Talk about the ways you've handled arguments as a couple in the past. What was it like in the dating stage? What effect did marriage have, if any, on the way you have disagreed? Here's your assignment: Both of you should name your own worst tendency in handling conflict—talk about yourself, not your partner. What is it about your problem-solving skills that could use a little spiritual growth?

Then each of you should complete this sentence: The next time we argue, I'm going to try my hardest to _____. Then affirm and encourage one another before praying together, thanking God for the amazing power of grace he has given us for fighting the evil of bitterness.

Next Verse: **Hebrews 12:14–15**

DAY 5
What I Like About You
Song of Solomon 7:1

Answer this one: What was the happiest moment you've ever experienced in the workplace?

According to study after study, most people answer that question differently than you might expect. They don't name the time they got the raise or the promotion. What they like to talk about is the occasion when someone said, "Good work! You really did that well." It's emotionally far more pleasurable than anything else we could receive on the job.

Positive words carry awesome power. And it's even truer in marriage. Negative words—nagging, criticism—kill intimacy. Positive ones nurture it. We need to work at using uplifting language with each other. Let me give you a valuable tip in this regard: When your spouse comes and tells you some good news, don't smile and say, "Hey, that's nice." Dr. Shelly Gable, a UCLA researcher, says you ought to be more demonstrative. Hug. Offer a kiss. Jump up and down a little bit. Dr. Gable says that when we celebrate our partner's victory, we build intimacy in an incredible way. The message your spouse receives: My victory is your victory. You love me that much.

Another specialist (they do all kinds of cool studies, don't they?) tells us that happily married couples show a ratio of five positive verbal and emotional responses to every negative one; struggling marriages show less than a one-to-one ratio.

This week we've talked about conflict. Positive and encouraging words are the best strategy for working out solutions, but they're also preventive maintenance. Your marriage should be constantly "under construction," with each of you building up the other. A marriage that has built a foundation with positive encouragement will stand strong against the conflict storms that will inevitably come.

After Mr. and Mrs. Solomon had their spat, they came to the fun part—
making up:

How beautiful your sandaled feet, O prince's daughter!
Your graceful legs are like jewels, the work of an artist's hands.

– Song of Solomon 7:1

It's interesting to compare the words in the seventh chapter to those in
the fourth. They're very similar. The couple has returned to the love talk
they used in courting and on their first night together.

It feels good to make things right. The storm has passed and our tone
softens. We use words to express what is so hard to find words for: the love
we feel. We use the words I'm sorry, and we seal it with a kiss—or perhaps
more. Physical love is a powerful symbol that we are still one flesh.

But don't save encouraging words for after the battle! Affirming words are
even more powerful when nothing's been broken and nobody is upset.
How about a phone call during the day for no other reason than to say,
"I'm thinking of you"? How about flowers and a poem on some day that
isn't Valentine's Day, a birthday, or an anniversary? How about finding
something you've never praised your spouse for?

THE BRIDGE
Which of you does the better job offering encouraging words? What
kinds of things are the subjects of these statements?

Here's something you'll enjoy. Ask God to help you see the wonderful
things about your spouse through new eyes during the next few days—
that's going to mean being observant and insightful on your part. Romans 12:10 says, "Be devoted to one another in love. Honor one another
above yourselves." But some translations such as the English Standard
Version have that last phrase as "outdo one another in showing honor."

That's what I want you to do. Find opportunities during the next few days to show honor and devotion through positive, encouraging words. Be creative in how you express your thoughts, and be sincere—no bland, general compliments. Be specific! Tell why you love that trait in your spouse. And watch as Christ knits the two of you closer together in intimacy.

Next Verse: **Romans 12:10**

NOTES:

WEEK **4** REDISCOVERING
ROMANCE

ROMANCE

DAY 1
Silly Love Songs
Song of Solomon 7:1–9

How does a culture define love? One way to answer that question is to listen to the music. The majority of popular songs are about love—which shows you how important it is to us. The titles can be very revealing, particularly about the period of time that produced that song.

So why not have a little fun with that idea? All of the little ditties below are real songs—some you'll recognize; others will make you say, "Really?" Just match the titles on the left to the correct year on the right. Your prize is the comfortable knowledge that you're a king of pop-culture trivia.

1. "Love Is Atomic"	a. 1912
2. "Justify My Love"	b. 1983
3. "A Groovy Kind of Love"	c. 2001
4. "Love Is Like a Shoogy Shoo"	d. 1938
5. "Love Is a Battlefield"	e. 1990
6. "Falling in Love with Love"	f. 1965

Answers: 1.(c); 2.(e); 3.(f); 4.(a); 5.(b); 6.(d).

In Song of Solomon, we've seen the couple's first rough moment. Last week we noted in 7:1 how Solomon used the language of praise and affirmation with his wife. He made all the right moves to get their relationship on track:

How beautiful your sandaled feet, O prince's daughter! Your graceful legs are like jewels, the work of an artist's hands.

– Song of Solomon 7:1

Honeymoon forgiveness is one thing, but what about years later? What about those occasions in a mature marriage when we can't seem to find that old romantic feeling?

Let's note two truths. First, just as Solomon took the lead here, it's best for men to make the first move in reconciliation. That's tough for many proud guys, but it's the right thing to do.

Second, let's recognize that this is an issue in every marriage. We simply can't maintain that intense, honeymoon, emotional dynamic or we'd burn out! We'd get little done at work or anywhere else. Some of that old romantic sizzle is going to leak away, and that's not completely a bad thing—we have other business in life to attend to. Still, marriage requires maintenance. We need to be proactive in keeping the home fires burning.

This week we'll learn from Solomon's wisdom about doing that.

THE BRIDGE
Read the first nine verses of Song of Solomon 7 with your spouse. What song title would best describe your current romantic status? (You don't have to choose one of the titles above.) Talk about the time when you first met and fell in love. Compare your romantic feelings. How did each of you express them? Over time, how have you maintained this aspect of your love? In what ways have you seen it subside?

Here's some advice you're not going to hear me give: "Feel romantic again today." Feelings can't be commanded; they're the emotions that come naturally as the result of actions and observations. Maybe you've heard the phrase, "Fake it until you make it." It's possible to act your way into a feeling. So don't beat yourselves up if those old crazy feelings aren't there. Instead, simply spend some time reminiscing about those great times when you first got together. Speak in particular about the wonderful things in your spouse that made you feel the way you did. The emotions that result might surprise you.

Next Verse: **1 Peter 4:8**

DAY 2
You Are So Beautiful to Me
Song of Solomon 7:6

Extreme Makeover was a reality-TV hit. The producers promised to take ordinary people and transform their appearance. Deleese Williams, a wife and mother from Texas, was one of those. She was set to receive "the works," and her family was coached to focus on her supposed ugliness in advance interviews. This would make everything more dramatic.

Except the episode never happened. A dental surgeon counseled that the time required for his work wouldn't fit the network timetable, so Deleese was sent home the day before her big day of procedures.

The problem was, she didn't want to go home—not after so much emphasis on her "ugliness." Not after all those interviews she'd heard. Deleese Williams sunk into depression and refused to leave her home except for grocery shopping at midnight. Meanwhile, her sister, mortified over the words she'd been prompted to say on TV, took her own life. "The family is shredded," said a spokesman.

It was more reality than TV wanted.

When we look at our spouse, or anyone else, we usually see whatever it is we are looking for. Nothing destroys romance more quickly than a critical eye that is always pointing out the ugly. Mr. and Mrs. Solomon were careful to notice the beauty in one another.

How beautiful you are and how pleasing, my love, with your delights!

– Song of Solomon 7:6

Our culture places extreme value on looks, as carefully defined by an army of models and movie stars. It's fine to talk about beauty being skin-deep, but we internalize our cultural values all the same. Every single one of us wants to believe we look good, that we are beautiful in the eyes of others. And we yearn to hear the words.

Part of rekindling romance is simply saying, "You are lovely to me." In Song of Solomon chapter 7, the husband praised his wife for her beauty, her character, and for the way she delighted him. It sounds pretty basic, doesn't it? Yet how often do we let our loved ones become invisible? He loves her; he just didn't notice her new hairstyle. She hasn't noticed that he's been losing weight through jogging. We see them so much we don't really see them, and we stop noticing their beauty.

We should be students of our life partners, noticing everything about them and celebrating it whenever we can. What's the most basic difference between now and the time when you first fell in love? Words. You spoke the words of love. Nothing escaped your notice.

Let your spouse know he or she still turns you on. Point out the little examples of excellence, good character, and the distinctive laugh or special smile that lights you up even today. Romance is rekindled when we express our attraction to each other.

THE BRIDGE

Beauty. Character. Delight.

These are three traits singled out by Solomon as he praised his bride. Why not give it a whirl? Talk to each other about why you like the way your mate looks, some of the things you like about your mate's character in everyday situations, and finally, some of the many little things you find delightful and endearing. Do it wholeheartedly! Don't be afraid to fly the flag of your love for your favorite human being. Since God loves for us to encourage one another, he'll suggest things to you as you speak, things you might not have thought of before. You may be a little out of practice, but it will come back to you.

Another suggestion: Put it in writing. Later on, write some of these down and give the note to your spouse to keep. Every now and then you need to renew these thoughts together.

Finally, pray as a couple. Thank God for the blessings he has given you through the life mate he sent you, and ask him to help you make a habit out of praise and encouragement. Ask him to help you have eyes to see the beauty in your spouse.

Next Verse: **Philippians 4:8**

NOTES:

_____
_____
_____
_____
_____
_____
_____
_____
_____
_____
_____

DAY 3
You Make Me Feel Brand New
Song of Solomon 7:13

The Museum of Broken Relationships. That's not some high-flown metaphor; it's a thing. Two artists in Zagreb, Croatia, founded the museum after their four-year relationship ended badly. I guess they broke up, they were dividing their stuff, and they realized that every item told a story.

Thus began the Museum of Broken Relationships. Visitors are invited to bring souvenirs of their own pain. You might see a pot or pan that was embedded in the wall after a bad fight or a lawn gnome someone ran over while screeching away in the car. There's some truly sad creativity: A woman ordered a twenty-fifth anniversary cake and cut it in half to symbolize their broken marriage. The kids could "choose a side" of the cake to eat from.

Strange that people could be as creative in falling out of love as they were falling into it. Why can't we use some imagination in the midst of marriage, when it really counts? When is the last time you creatively and thoughtfully put effort into winning the heart of your spouse?

The mandrakes send out their fragrance, and at our door is every delicacy, both new and old, that I have stored up for you, my beloved.

– Song of Solomon 7:13

As we reach the next few verses, the wife now began to speak, responding to Solomon, who had lavished her with words of love. She responded with creativity, spontaneity, and an aggressive spirit. Men love that in women! She spoke up. She wanted to try new things. Specifically, she referred to sexual love in these verses, offering delicacies "both new and old." Using double meanings, she said, "Let's go do some gardening. I have some of your favorite greens—and a couple new ones that will knock your socks off."

Yes, I hear men complain that women are reluctant to try new things in this area. I also know they're more likely to respond, as Solomon's wife did, to loving attention and language. A husband needs to be more assertive in expressing his love and a wife needs to be more responsive. Part of rekindling the romance in marriage is simply being willing to break out of old ruts, showing we care enough about each other to work on making everything better. This isn't just a question of the bedroom, of course. We need to be spontaneous, creative, and proactive in finding new ways to make our love new again.

THE BRIDGE

Do I have to paint you a picture? I think you get the general drift of all this. Spend time talking as a couple about ruts today. Somebody said a rut is a coffin with the ends kicked out. It takes a little effort to get out of the doldrums, but once you have, it feels good.

Talk about ways you can change things up. What's some "new" that you can add to the relationship? Just as God's tender mercies are new every morning, we should be tender with one another in new ways every day. The verse below, as a matter of fact, is an invitation to think about how God "woos" us.

Love is worth it; your spouse is worth it. You might say, "I'm not the creative type; I don't know what to do." Ask God to help you be more romantic, spontaneous, and creative as a couple. Like nearly anything else, it's simply a daily discipline of learning to think of ways to bless each other.

Next Verse: **Jeremiah 31:3**

DAY 4
Come Go With Me
Song of Solomon 7:11

Same ol' same ol'. He would get home from his job and she'd get home from hers every Friday night. One of them would shrug and ask, "Same ol' same ol'?" The other would say, "I guess." And they'd go to the mall. There they could order their dinners of choice at the food court. Then he could go and shop for stuff he needed; she could shop for her own. "Date night" had all the sparkle of a dust ball. Sometimes they would get really crazy and make an unplanned stop at the grocery store on the way home.

Then, last Friday, they were standing in the doorway when he asked the usual question: "Same ol' same ol'?"
"No," she said. "This time we visit a restaurant that's new to us—with a kind of cooking we've been afraid to try. But we go there after."
"After what?"
"The mall, as usual," she said, "except we're shaking things up. I'm shopping for you, and you're shopping for me."
"But . . ."
"We buy each other a gift. Under forty dollars."
He sweated a little, but it all worked out. They had a blast exchanging gifts. He got her a really cool case for her computer tablet—just the kind of thing she'd never have splurged to buy for herself. And she bought him some new golf gloves: "I think those ragged ones you were using belonged to your grandfather." They had a terrific dinner of really strange cuisine neither of them liked—or noticed.

Come, my beloved, let us go to the countryside, let us spend the night in the villages.

– Song of Solomon 7:11

Again the wife was being assertive in an appealing way. Her husband had taken the lead in being loving and she responded with creativity and energy. "Let's go somewhere!" she was saying. "Let's go to the country, where it's beautiful, and find some rustic place to spend the night." This, of course, is another secret of couples who keep the fire going in their marriage. They understand that travel wakes us up in a special way. It pulls away all the distractions—work, home entertainment, even the kids—and brings us together in experiencing something new.

The idea of going somewhere is always exciting, but the real agenda is not the place but the person. The wife made that clear throughout this passage. Her feet may have wandered, but her eyes were only for him.

THE BRIDGE

When was the last time you got away just to get away? I'm not talking about planned vacations but a spontaneous "let's disappear together" moment, a quick weekend at a bed-and-breakfast or a trip to the lake, just the two of you. Vacations can actually be stressful and overplanned. We tend to go places and put our focus on the destination. The idea here is to get away from the same ol' same ol' and mix it up so you can focus on each other.

So talk about that, pray about that today. Get your calendars out. Plan a time for a romantic getaway with the commitment of enjoying each other to the utmost. Warning: That might mean leaving the laptop computer at home. It might actually mean putting away your cell phone for a while. It may mean leaving your kids for a night or two. Devote yourselves to each other, and watch your love grow deeper.

Next Verse: **1 Thessalonians 4:9**

DAY 5
You're My Everything
Song of Solomon 7:10

I remember the early days of our marriage. We had just moved away from my hometown and headed west to start a new church in California. It was exciting and challenging and I talked with my dad almost every day about what was happening. He has always been a mentor to me and I greatly valued his opinion.

One day my wife walked into the room as I was talking to Dad on the phone. I was getting his thoughts on some things going on at work. When I wrapped up the conversation, DesiRae asked me about the things she'd heard me discussing. "Why haven't you talked about that with me?" she asked. "I don't know. I guess I meant to," I said. "I think it's great that you talk to your dad about everything that's going on, but I want to be a part of it as well."

Wow. I had honestly never thought about how I was making her feel. "Honor your father and mother" is so ingrained in us that we tend to forget another verse—one in Genesis about leaving and cleaving unto your new spouse. Or maybe you have a somewhat codependent relationship with Mom or Dad that has kept you from the depth of love God wants you to experience in marriage.

I've seen this happen a lot over the years. People get married, but they don't quite cut the apron strings. Numerous times I have said to a husband, "I'm glad you love and honor your mom, but you need to love and honor your wife more." There is nothing more romantic than two lives joining together as one, but that doesn't happen unless both the husband and wife give all of who they are to one another.

I belong to my beloved, and his desire is for me.

– Song of Solomon 7:10

Rekindling romance requires a strong emotional connection. Marriage is a oneness, a unity of spirit created by God. Sexual love, becoming one flesh, is the physical symbol of it. But we also experience an incredible unity through a deep emotional connection.

Sometimes we make the terrible mistake of allowing other relationships to be more important than the relationship with our spouse. Sometimes it's your parents. Sometimes it's your friendships. Sometimes it's your coworkers. Sometimes it's your clients. Or maybe it's your children. They take the place of your spouse when it comes to your attention and affection.

No one can or should replace a spouse. When your husband or wife is not your truest earthly connection, something has gone wrong.

Solomon's wife expressed her oneness with her lover in 7:10. They had belonging, and therefore they had desire. That word desire has a meaning in the original language of "consuming." We feel a hunger, both sexually and emotionally, for each other. Truly married people don't look forward to being away from each other. When they're not together, the world isn't right. They have that incredible connection that causes them to complete each other's sentences, and as they grow old, sometimes people insist they even start to look alike!

THE BRIDGE

Today's assignment is a little more demanding. Spend some time together reflecting on your emotional connection. Be honest and transparent. How close are you these days? Has there been any drifting away? When is the last time you felt truly connected? What can you do to restore the emotional connection that is so necessary? How often do the two of you take a long walk and have a good talk? Identity the obstacles to your unity.

This is another one of those prayers that you can be absolutely certain God will answer: "Lord, bind us closer." The trick is, you'll need to pray it more than once. If you realize that God needs to do some repair and remodeling in your marriage, you need to be praying it every day—not alone but together. And thank him in advance for the miracles he is about to do.

Next Verse: **Philippians 4:6–7**

NOTES:

WEEK **5** CULTIVATING COMMITMENT

COMMITMENT

DAY 1
If I Fell
Song of Solomon 8:9

"Free at last!" I was at the gym when I heard him say it, laughing with his workout buddy. I was on the next machine, puffing and straining, and it was impossible not to hear the conversation. He was getting a divorce. I was fascinated by the celebratory tone. Divorce is no trip to the carnival. I've counseled a countless number of people who were devastated by the pain of a breakup. I understood, of course, that this gym guy's laughter was only on the outside. It's just a macho thing to try to seem bulletproof.

I walked over and said, "Excuse me, I'm not nosy—it's just that I was right over there and couldn't help hearing that you're going through a divorce." He nodded and I could tell he wasn't the kind of person who felt awkward very easily. I went on, "I was just wondering if there was anything I could do to help. I'm a pastor and a pretty decent listener. I also know that sometimes it's easier to tell certain things to someone you don't know. Maybe it's not too late for you guys."

So we talked for a few minutes. Basically his story had two parts: (1) We fell in love and (2) we fell out of love.

And that was about it. I wish this story had a happily-ever-after ending, but he was sure there was someone else out there who would make him happy. Somehow, in a time when most of us feel we're in charge of our own lives, we believe love just floats in on its own and then goes away mysteriously, and there's not too much anybody can do about it. Fall in, fall out.

How did we ever fall for such an idea?

If she is a wall, we will build towers of silver on her.

If she is a door, we will enclose her with panels of cedar.

– Song of Solomon 8:9

Families in the time of Solomon took marriage very seriously. As in many cultures, the match was arranged from the time of the couple's childhood. Elaborate ceremonies filled with symbolism were held. Parents mentored the bride and groom, preparing them for life as a married couple. Divorce was necessary even to break the engagement or betrothal.

Purity at the time of the wedding—that is, virginity—was serious business. In Song of Solomon 8:9, another young lady was being discussed. What is this talk of walls and doors? (People don't say many things directly in this book, do they?)

"If she is a wall," she is closed, sturdy; she is pure. A swinging door, of course, is just the opposite; the young woman is unchaste. The "wall" is an honorable structure, one for building "towers of silver." Men and women of character become the foundations of great families. Their marriages don't come tumbling down when the first storm hits.

Now compare those towers of old to these "swinging" times of today. No wonder people are "falling" in and out of love, stumbling through one door and out the next.

THE BRIDGE

Divorce is not the unforgivable sin. It's actually one more opportunity for God to show his healing power. But we'd rather show his power through a marriage built to last, a marriage that rises into the sky like a turret with a flag waving at the top. People see it and say, "Those are people of God."

This week's topic is commitment. Are you building a tower or a revolving door? Talk about what that commitment means to each of you. How is your commitment to God related to your commitment to each other? Pray that God will continue to build "towers of silver" through your marriage partnership, and thank him for being the architect of eternal things. If you haven't been building "towers of silver," pray that God will take the broken pieces and make it stronger than ever. Remember, he can redeem anything.

Next Verse: **1 Peter 2:5**

DAY 2
My One and Only
Song of Solomon 8:4

Since 1990, the percentage of couples living together before marriage has nearly doubled. Hardly anyone bats an eye anymore at the idea of "moving in together."

Obviously, the idea of sex before marriage is no longer a cultural taboo. You could almost argue the reverse—that couples delaying sex until marriage are considered strange and old-fashioned. I bet you've heard this argument: "You wouldn't want to buy a car without taking it for a test drive, right?"

When you first hear it, there seems to be a kind of logic. Sure, "try before you buy" is usually a good policy. Take that car for a spin, find the open highway, and push the pedal to the floor. But since we're comparing it with marriage, you don't keep the car for just half an hour, right? You drive it for a good while. You put some miles on it. You wear down the tires and maybe you leave some trash in the car before turning it in. "I thought this was the car for me," you say, "but I'm tired of it. I'd like to see a newer model."

That's the thing. The test-drive analogy sounds great if you're the driver, but if you're the car, not so much. Once the other person walks away, you don't feel as if you're behind the wheel anymore. You just feel used.

Daughters of Jerusalem, I charge you:

Do not arouse or awaken love until it so desires.

– Song of Solomon 8:4

As discussed yesterday, Hebrew culture had an intense view of wedding preparation. If you think today's weddings get complicated, you'd be shocked by what went on in Solomon's day.

The season of betrothal lasted no less than a year. The wedding was a destination that was reached with a lot of work. While the chathan (groom) and kallâ (bride) would spend a great deal of time with their parents learning about the importance of the institution of marriage, the bride's chastity was basically kept under heavy guard.

There was a contract. There was a dowry, a gift presented by the groom to the bride's father in appreciation. A dash of wine poured by the groom and sipped by the bride sealed the deal—and the mothers smashed plates on the ground. Why? The plates meant that this thing was as final as broken china. Marriage was meant to be forever.

This is why the bride said not to awaken love until the time was right. So many things depend on cooperating with God's timing. We can't be so casual about this subject. Otherwise we don't end up with broken plates; we end up with broken families and broken hearts.

THE BRIDGE

I know you're getting the message that nothing in this life is more important than your relationship with your marriage partner—nothing other than God himself. You get that. But if you're married, isn't it a little late to be talking about sexual purity and preparation for marriage?

Maybe it's too late to change how we prepared for marriage, but it's important to recognize God's way and repent of ignoring the standards he established. The Bible says in James that we should repent and confess our sins so that we can experience healing. Repent of the sin in your marriage and ask God to heal the brokenness.

I also encourage you to pray for other couples you know who may be struggling to keep their commitment. Statistics tell us that our churches are filled with struggling marriages. My wife and I have found that one of the most effective ways to cultivate commitment in our marriage is to reach out and encourage couples who are engaged or newly married and feeling somewhat disillusioned.

Solomon's bride went out of her way to pass along godly counsel to the Daughters of Jerusalem. Make an effort to pray for and encourage other married couples and you may find it strengthens your own marriage.

Next Verse: Proverbs 5:18–19

NOTES:

Day 3
Signed, Sealed, Delivered
Song of Solomon 8:6

I visited my hometown not too long ago.

It's always terrific seeing everybody. My cousin and I spent some time with Grandma. We all climbed into the car and drove to the cemetery to visit Grandpa's grave.

There's a special brand of quiet in a graveyard. So many lives gathered in silence. I glanced at my grandmother's face and saw the thoughtful look of yearning on her face. I thought to myself, She's still married to him.

Sixty years they were together in marriage. Death is an ominous punctuation mark, but after that long together, you're no less married. The headstone next to Grandpa's was blank. We knew this spot was reserved for her. Yet a place in Grandma's bed was blank, too. She told us how she'd find herself reaching over to touch him in the darkness, just sure he'd be there. She'd call for him in the next room, certain he'd appear in the doorway.

Some commitments are so strong that death itself can't break them. Physically we may be apart, but spiritually and emotionally, the connection is alive and powerful.

Place me like a seal over your heart, like a seal on your arm; for love is as strong as death, its jealousy unyielding as the grave. It burns like blazing fire, like a mighty flame.

– Song of Solomon 8:6

"Love is as strong as death." Wow. That may be the most powerful sentence in Solomon's book of love—especially when you understand the imagery in these words. A seal was generally a ring you pushed into clay to make an impression. It left a mark that said, "Mine; hands off forever." You didn't place a seal on something that wasn't valuable.

But notice that Solomon's wife herself was a seal: "Place me like a seal over your heart." It's all part of the oneness, the one-flesh nature of marriage.

That's why it's as strong as death, as unyielding as the grave. Jealousy comes from the same root as zealous. If anyone else tries to take my place with my wife, you'd better believe I'd be jealous—righteously jealous. Because I'm zealous, committed, sold out for her love.

THE BRIDGE

The wedding ceremony is all about marking this relationship as permanent—setting a seal on each other: Signed, sealed, delivered, I'm yours. But what's more important is that the marriage itself be all about that. Do you have a forever mentality in your marriage? Has "Till death do us part" become woven into the fabric of your relationship? Truly married couples don't think, "I can live with this person"; they think, "I can't live without this person."

It's fascinating to me that just as we set a seal on one another's hearts, the New Testament speaks of God setting his own seal upon us (see Ephesians 1:13). Marriage is a reflection of the love of God. Decide that the word divorce will not be in your vocabulary. You are united as one and you cannot consider life without your spouse any more than you would consider life without your arms or legs.

Talk about the seal on your hearts today—about growing old together, about caring for one another, even as health declines for one or both of you. What will be the rewards of staying together for the long haul? In what ways has your sense of commitment increased and your love deepened since the wedding? Ask God to strengthen that seal.

Next Verse: **Ephesians 1:13**

DAY 4
Light My Fire
Song of Solomon 8:7

Connubial bliss. You've got to love that phrase—it's the old-school way of saying, "happily married." Call it whatever you want; we were young, newly married, and connubiality was way blissful.

We had friends named Jim and Judy whom we really admired. Jim got a rough medical report: lung cancer. When we stopped in to pray with them, we saw how strong the cancer was—and how their faith was even stronger. The most aggressive chemotherapy was being used, along with radiation treatments. But Jim was becoming very weak and feeble.

One evening I was in his room reading Scripture when the smell made it clear he'd lost bowel control. Judy said, "Excuse us for a minute," and we waited outside while she cleaned up. As she came back to get us, there was a smile on her face that I'll never forget. "In sickness and in health," she said.

That was an education for the two of us, young and healthy and in love. It's one thing to stand at the altar and say those words along with, "Till death do us part." Would we still say it if we could look into the future and know what was in store? (Song of Solomon 8:6) says
The next verse:

Many waters cannot quench love; rivers cannot sweep it away. If one were to give all the wealth of one's house for love, it would be utterly scorned.

– Song of Solomon 8:7

Again, I find it fascinating to spot a parallel with the way God's Spirit seals us—fire is always a symbol for the Spirit of God.

I know there's a love in our marriage that seals us; I know that it's a flame that will not be extinguished in this lifetime. We won't "fall out of love." Not likely. But I will say this: We intend to provide plenty of kindling.

That's how you make a fire greater and warmer and more powerful.

Many waters—not any waters—cannot quench the love that God builds in us. The waters of cancer won't do it. The waters of aging and losing our looks won't do it. The waters of extramarital temptation or pornography or disagreements or simple stress—go ahead and bring those buckets. We know they're coming, and we know our love and our faith are more than a match for them.

THE BRIDGE

Solomon's bride added one other thought: Not only is love a fire you can't extinguish, it's a treasure you can't purchase. All wealth would be scorned.

In other words, money can't buy me love. What can? Commitment. First to God and then to each other. Today I suggest you find the buckets. Talk about the cold water that is being thrown on your relationship. Where are those buckets coming from?

Name as many "buckets" as you can and pray about them. Realize that no matter what they are—even if they're the very threat of death—your Lord and your love for each other will keep the fire burning.

Talking about it and praying about it is the beginning of adding kindling to your fire, of "fanning it into flame," in the words of Paul to Timothy. Here's to plenty of heat and light in your time together.

Next Verse: **2 Timothy 1:6**

DAY 5
I Can't Get No Satisfaction
Song of Solomon 8:10

You'd never have known he was a world-record holder. Glynn Wolfe died alone at eighty-eight years old. Like many forgotten people, he was buried in an unmarked grave at the city's expense. It happens, sadly enough.

The odd thing is that Wolfe was the most married man in the world—in a manner of speaking. According to the Guinness Book of World Records, he was a veteran of twenty-nine marriages. I'm not sure what wedding vows were his favorite, but "till death do us part" doesn't seem to have been part of his definition.

Surviving Wolfe were a good number of kids, grandkids, great-grandkids, and of course ex-wives and former in-laws—most of whom considered him an outlaw, apparently, because none of them came to bury him.

It's a pretty sad story, a sort of caricature of the restlessness people seem to have these days. They're always looking for the better job, the better house, the better spouse. They try something out, shake their heads with displeasure, and walk away. Because they feel entitled, it never occurs to them that the key to contentment may actually be within themselves.

I am a wall, and my breasts are like towers.

Thus I have become in his eyes like one bringing contentment.

– Song of Solomon 8:10

One of our biggest problems is that the search begins as early as it does. Keep in mind all that we've learned about marriage in Solomon's time—the measures taken to protect a young woman's purity. Then think about today.

What we call dating is a process that can go on for years and involve "trying on" many different relationships as if they were so many shoes.

People connect on deep and intimate levels and then break it off. What they're doing is giving away little pieces of themselves. Pieces of the heart are like pieces of a pie, if you want to think of it that way. If we give away enough of ourselves, what's left for the one we eventually marry? Solomon's bride returned to the language of walls and towers—images of sturdiness. He looked at her and saw a relationship built to last, and he was content.

Romance is nurtured by the feeling that God has given you a treasure and that you have the rest of your life to exult in that treasure. All the while, he is going to draw you closer each day. Together you'll take on every challenge life offers. Together: a beautiful word, one that brings contentment.

THE BRIDGE

Where do you stand in an age of restlessness? Are you content with your marriage? Your home? Your work? Your ministry for God?

We are commanded to be content. Hebrews 13:5 tells us to be content with what we have simply because God has told us he will never leave or forsake us. That should hold true of your partner. If you know your marriage is built to last, you can feel great peace and satisfaction—and get on with the work of serving him, loving each other, and building a family that will bless the world. Discontentment is the enemy of commitment.

Thanksgiving and gratitude creates a spirit of contentment, and contentment cultivates commitment. Pull out a piece of paper and make a list of all the things about your marriage you are thankful for.

Next Verse: **Philippians 4:12**

WEEK **6** FOSTERING
FAITH

FAITH

DAY 1
Love on a Two-Way Street
Psalm 127:1

I was sitting in a restaurant when I spotted a bored married couple. They ate silently, never looking at each other.

I thought, Is that where the road always leads? The place where you run out of things to talk about? Yet I read the following quotation by Andre Maurois: "A happy marriage is a long conversation which always seems too short." That's what I want; you too.

In physics, there's something called the law of entropy that says everything runs down. I own lots of electronics, and I could have told them that. The law goes on to say that unless new energy is introduced, any organism will eventually disintegrate.

I see entropic marriages, and you do too. They lack that "new energy," which, of course, is the presence and participation of God. When DesiRae and I were in premarriage counseling, we were shown a diagram of a triangle. At the bottom two points were husband and wife, and at the third point up top was Jesus. The counselor told us that the closer each of us drew to Jesus, the closer we would draw to each other. That has proven to be truer than I ever would have imagined.

Jesus is a source of life and love and adventure, a spring of living water that never runs dry. Without that point of the triangle, you're left with a line segment with two endpoints, a highway with two dead ends.

Unless the Lord builds the house, the builders labor in vain.

– Psalm 127:1

God's place in your marriage is the root issue. You can read all the books on marriage you want, go to marriage-enrichment seminars, and listen to self-help gurus or Dr. Phil. They'll all give you some helpful tips, but they won't cure the root issue. It's like our friend who had a serious lung disease. He might have taken cough syrup, and at first it might have made a difference. But ultimately he needed to confront the disease.

We're trying to build a home, and the psalm tells us there is only one architect whose plan will work, one landlord who can keep the building from falling into disrepair. Otherwise, the builders labor in vain. All the personal strategies and marriage tips in the world won't make a difference.

What do we know about Solomon, who has given us a window into the origins of his romance? We know God gave him great wisdom. We know he was an eloquent writer and poet, a great politician, a builder. He had a spiritual heart for God and a romantic heart for love. But it all came to deep heartbreak for him. God gave him specific advice about marriage, and he didn't take it (see 1 Kings 11:9). He married many wives, including some who brought pagan gods into the kingdom. In other words, he followed after the world of men rather the Word of God.

THE BRIDGE

This will be a week for taking stock of the spiritual foundation in your marriage. We'll look at several angles of that.

Today, let's think about Solomon's love story with a rather unhappy sequel. Once, he had eyes for only one woman; later, his eyes wandered. This doesn't have to be a matter of adultery but can be any other false god we bring into the place that God has said must be holy and committed to him. Do you see any false gods on the horizon of your marriage? They may come in many clever disguises. Is something or someone other than Jesus the foundation you are building your marriage and family upon?

Next Verse: **1 John 1:7**

DAY 2
Something about You
1 John 4:16–17

It was a typical business seminar: a big room full of guys on expense accounts, eager to see who could act the most like an aged-out frat boy. One guy seemed kind of quiet, though. He sat in a corner and read during coffee breaks.

Several women had been sent by their companies, and one was particularly attractive. She could have been a model, but here she was at an information-technology conference. Naturally, the guys had her in their sights within seconds. They were competing to get the seat beside her, find out which restaurant she'd chosen for dinner, and be the first to get her room number.

Finally, one of the guys caught the eye of the attractive woman. She smiled and patted the seat next to her. The guy rushed to her side as his competitors sighed. "I've been wanting to talk to you," she said. "Oh, me too!" the guy said, trying to hold back the drool.

"I saw you come in with that guy," she said, pointing at the reading guy in the corner. "You must be in his business group. It looks like he and I use the same Bible translation. Any way I can get an introduction?"

God is love. Whoever lives in love lives in God, and God in them. This is how love is made complete among us.

– 1 John 4:16–17

You've seen too many movies. So have I. We've picked up certain ideas about what attracts the opposite sex. For instance, women are supposed to be attracted to "the rebel." The guy once played by James Dean in the movies, the guy who plays the game by his own rules.

Actually, not so much. Characters like that are nice to visit for ninety minutes in a dark theater or on a DVD, but who wants to build a life with a guy who can't be trusted and has a good chance of ending up on America's Dumbest Criminals?

The truth is that within marriage both sides are attracted to godly character. It only sounds strange because it doesn't sell in Hollywood or on women's magazine covers. We see in our mate what our heart knows we need the most. And if it happens that both of us are seeking Christ, the effect is magnified. Our attraction to Christ enhances our attraction to each other.

Remember the triangular marriage diagram? If both of us are moving up the line that leads toward Christ, what happens geometrically? The two points move closer and closer together. Think about that the next time a little voice whispers that it's a waste of time to pray together or study Scripture together.

THE BRIDGE

Yesterday we talked about the things that tear us apart: elements of this world that take God's place in our marriages. Today we're talking about the ideal, the opposite. Any marriage, even a dying one, can become loving and dynamic if both partners are pursuing Christ together. It's just not possible that Christ would lead them away from each other.

How do you follow Jesus together in your marriage? It's important to have private devotions and a personal relationship with Christ, but you also need to have a shared relationship. Discuss and pray about ways the two of you can begin growing closer to Christ as a couple. Talk about a plan for how both of you individually and together will follow hard after Jesus.

Next Verse: **Hosea 2:19–20**

DAY 3

Stout-Hearted Men

1 Corinthians 11:3

She is a best-selling Christian author who has influenced millions. But years ago Liz Curtis Higgs lived a life that was the polar opposite. She was a crass radio personality who would never have described herself as a Christian. She was a single feminist who led a pretty wild life. And then one weekend many years ago, long before I was a part of things, she reluctantly agreed to visit the church where I am now a pastor. She didn't want to go, but she knew it was the only way to get her friends to stop asking. The first weekend she came, the pastor, Bob Russell, was preaching through Ephesians and just happened to be preaching a sermon on wives submitting to their husbands. Liz's friends couldn't believe that of the weekends Bob would preach on this passage it would be the weekend she came to church. They were sure she would never come back. But then Bob got to the part in the passage about husbands loving their wives and being willing to die for them. Liz says at that moment she leaned over and joked to her friend, "If I ever met a man who'd die for me, I'd marry him in a minute." Her friend whispered back, "Oh, Lizzy, there is a man who loves you so much that he has already died for you."

But I want you to realize that the head of every man is Christ, and the head of the woman is man, and the head of Christ is God.

– 1 Corinthians 11:3

The idea of the husband as spiritual leader bothers some people who get hung up on "who's the boss." It's not like that; biblical leadership is not demanding or harsh but loving and inviting. The man says, "Come with me, and let's go on the adventure of following Christ together. And I would lay down my life for you as Christ would for the church."

How many women come to me complaining that their husband provides too much spiritual leadership? Not too many. It's the opposite. "My husband won't take charge." That's what I hear over and over.

Men don't lead for any number of reasons. Some have bitterness issues within the marriage that need to be resolved before the two of them can take each other's hand and get going. Some men have never been shown by their own fathers how to lead spiritually. Many feel unworthy, not realizing that God will work through them; their wives, they think, simply know them too well. Some men feel so criticized by their wives that they are sure any attempt at spiritual leadership would end with a negative critique.

Some men have simply never made a start and don't know how to do so. Finally, and this is very important, we can't lead anyone to a place we're not heading. If a man has no relationship with Christ, how can he show the way for his wife and children? Ultimately I think this is what it comes down to for most husbands: you can't lead your wife to a place you're not going.

THE BRIDGE

Guys, this is your spotlight day. (Your wife gets her turn tomorrow.) How are you doing as a spiritual leader? I'm going to assume that if you're involved in week six of this study, you must be doing something right. What fears remain? How could you improve your performance?

Wives, this is an opportunity to be lovingly honest, constructive, and encouraging. Speak the truth compassionately. Pray together and ask for new breakthroughs in loving leadership by your husband. Find ways to affirm his leadership efforts.

Next Verse: **Ephesians 5:28**

DAY 4
The Wind beneath My Wings
Proverbs 31:25–26

The movie *42* told the amazing story of Jackie Robinson, who broke the color barrier in Major League Baseball in the 1940s. It's almost impossible for us to imagine how much courage it took for him to endure the constant racial taunting by other players, the shunning of teammates, and the torrent of threatening hate mail that arrived every day—threatening his safety, threatening his young family.

It's doubtful he would have made it without the encouragement of Rachel Robinson, his wife. She could have said, "I didn't sign up for this," and walked away. Instead, she gave the love and courage he needed to persevere. She helped draw up rules for surviving the death threats and daily vitriol. Home would be a place of love, refuge, and peace.

Her instincts were to protect her husband. She attended every home game so that he could always look up and see his wife in the bleachers. And on the way home they'd debrief, get it all out. That way, once they turned the doorknob and stepped into the house, there was no agenda but to rest and rejuvenate for the next battle.

I've found in ministry that there is rarely a leader who stands alone. Somewhere in his shadow you'll always find one very powerful woman whose encouragement fuels his every achievement. I could get a hundred pats on the back and encouraging comments, but no one breathes life into me as my wife does. Encouraging words from her are like oxygen for me.

She is clothed with strength and dignity; she can laugh at the days to come. She speaks with wisdom, and faithful instruction is on her tongue.

– Proverbs 31:25–26

Husbands are called to be spiritual leaders, but I believe the great spiritual mission of a wife in marriage is to be the spiritual encourager. I love the

Greek word parakaleo because it has so many shades of meaning. It is "to come alongside"; "to speak instruction, comfort, consolation, exhortation"; "to advocate or help." But most of all, we translate the word as "encourage."

In the New Testament, the Holy Spirit's name is parakletos because he does all these things for every Christian. And it is the special assignment of the wife to be the family parakletos, comforting, exhorting, encouraging, and coming alongside her husband and her children to give them new strength.

I believe many wives don't understand how deeply their husbands crave the encouragement of their wives. He comes home weary, used up, and discouraged, though he may do everything possible to hide it. He wants more than he even realizes: to be heard, to be cherished, to be the object of her pride.

This doesn't mean a lot of empty sunshine and flowers, but simply a reminder that one person in all the world is there for him no matter what the road holds. To know that she is there, standing in his corner, cheering him on, excited about his world, makes all the difference for him.

THE BRIDGE

Women, today is your day. How are you doing as an encourager? How does that role fit your personality and gifts? What do you find hardest about carrying out that task over time?

Guys, if you need more or if there are certain things you'd like to see, today is your chance. Talk to your wife in plain language, using the "drive-through window" law as your guide. (You have to clearly say what you want to get what you need.) You may be surprised how much it means to her that you long for her to be proud of you.

Today, pray for each other. He needs to thank God for his encourager, affirm her work, and ask God to bless her as she does it. She needs to thank God for a spiritual leader who is working to be the best he can be, and to ask for God's wisdom.

Next Verse: **Hebrews 3:13**

DAY 5
My Heart Will Go On
Psalm 127:3–5

If you don't know much about Jonathan Edwards, you need to change that. He was one of the greatest Americans and greatest Christians who ever lived.

Edwards, who lived in the 1700s, was a preacher, theologian, and the third president of Princeton University. He was at the center of the Great Awakening, a revival that turned the American colonies upside-down. Today people study his life almost as much as his teaching, because he was clearly an extraordinary man with an extraordinary marriage.

Sarah, his wife, bore him eleven children and managed an efficient home, though it was, at times, an impoverished one. The British evangelist George Whitefield was so impressed after a visit that he decided he needed to get married, too. Sarah outlived her husband by only six months.

In the year 1900, a scholar made a study of the descendants of Jonathan and Sarah Edwards. He found that the line included more than 100 lawyers, 30 judges, 13 college presidents, more than 100 professors, 60 doctors, and 100 pastors, missionaries, and theologians. There were 80 politicians, including 3 governors, several congressmen and senators, and a vice–president of the United States. There were 75 military officers, and the Edwards line published 135 books among 60 different authors. There seemed to be no trace of criminals.

Someday, up above, there will be one impressive family reunion.

Children are a heritage from the LORD, offspring a reward from him.

Like arrows in the hands of a warrior are children born in one's youth.

Blessed is the man whose quiver is full of them.

– Psalm 127:3–5

As we close out our study together, it's fitting to say a word about the future. We tend to get caught up in the moment, don't we? God designed humanity to live encased in one instant at a time, progressing through them toward an unknowable future.

Yet God promises wonderful things to those who are obedient, including married couples. Our children are only one example of that—but what an example. We can't have the details of the amazing things our kids and grandkids and great-grandkids will accomplish, but we know we're laying the groundwork by the way we live our lives right now.

It is our task to love one another and to build a great home. But the home is not an end itself. It is a living, thriving expression of the power of God in this world. It will reach out in every direction to make an impact, and it will reach into the future, beyond our own grasp. In this way, the decisions we make now have an exponential impact on the future and what God is laying out.

When you have one of those days, hold your spouse's hand. Remind each other that God is doing great works we can't even begin to imagine. In his power, your heart will go on.

THE BRIDGE
I hope this is not your final day of devotions together but a segue to many more. I've enjoyed sharing these thoughts and scriptural truths with you. Use today as a time of thanksgiving, praising God for the things you've learned and the plans he has through you. You might want to take a few moments to list your favorite insights from this study.

Spend some time asking God for his continued grace and mercy. All of our homes need lots of it. Pray with faith that God can and will restore and re-deem your marriage and family.

And, as always, pray for one another. Encourage one another. Walk in the light as he is in the light, and have fellowship with one another. Life is better together. Amen.

Next Verse: **Jeremiah 29:11**

NOTES:

NOTES: